Titles by *Langaa* RPCIG

The Barn

3 Plays by Kwo Victor Elame Musinga

Edited by Roselyne M. Jua

Langaa Research & Publishing CIG
Mankon, Bamenda

Publisher:
Langaa RPCIG
(*Langaa* Research & Publishing Common Initiative Group)
P.O. Box 902 Mankon
Bamenda
North West Province
Cameroon
Langaagrp@gmail.com
www.langaapublisher.com

Distributed outside N. America by African Books Collective
orders@africanbookscollective.com
www.africanbookscollective.com

Distributed in N. America by Michigan State University Press
msupress@msu.edu
www.msupress.msu.edu

ISBN: 9956-558-97-4

© Kwo Victor Elame Musinga & Roselyne M.Jua 2008

NJEMA, First Published 1984
An Invitation to God, First Published 2000
2 PLAYS, First Edition 2002, Second Edition 2003

To my children Barbara Balla Bokeng Musinga,
Carl Wase Sona Musinga, Isabella Fese Musinga
and all female students

Contents

Introduction to Kwo Victor Elame Musinga's *Njema,*
An Invitation to God and *Moka*
By *Francis B. Nyamnjoh*

It is my immense pleasure to write a brief introduction to *Njema, An Invitation to God* and *Moka*, three plays from the rich barn of the consummate and well-respected veteran playwright and actor, Kwo Victor Elame Musinga. My first encounter with Musinga was in 1975 when his Musinga Drama group visited Sacred Heart College Mankon, Bamenda, to perform *The Tragedy of Mr No Balance*, one of his early plays on bribery and corruption that has come to occupy the place of a classic in Cameroonian theatre in English. I was a Form Two student then, and privileged to be part of the audience of this first and only theatre evening in my five-year stay at the college. The performance was scintillating and I was so marked by the play and especially by Musinga's outstanding and very talented rendition of Mr No Balance, that in an English composition soon afterwards, I drew inspiration from the character, earning myself a distinction, something rather rare with me in those days. It is thanks in part to that early exposure to Musinga and his creative genius that I started toying with the idea of writing way back in secondary school. That I have since not given up is testimony to the need for early exposure to the possible influences that chart our destinies in writing and scholarship. This personal experience and vivid memory of the impact of *The Tragedy of Mr No Balance* on me as a thirteen year old, is indicative of the relevance and appeal of Musinga's plays to students and indeed to people of all ages and walks of life.

In *Njema* Musinga captures the predicament of love in a context where innocence and trust are preyed upon by deceit, dishonesty, promiscuity, waywardness, callous indifference to human life, the reckless abandon of parental authority and wisdom by youth in a hurry to celebrate sexuality, irresponsible manhood with or without the connivance of girls/women, and HIV/AIDS and its terror.

Through *Njema*, Musinga gives Cameroonians and human kind much food for thought: What hope is there for a society and its youth, when a girl turns down her mother's request to fetch water with the excuse that she is rushing to school (where, without her mother's knowledge, she has not been for almost a week despite similar rushes), only to head for an appointment "with her darling Aka," boasting how she put her mother "in her right place and disappeared"? What future is there for a society where men and women from childhood embrace promiscuity without responsibility, oblivious of the consequences in an era of HIV/AIDS and a multitude of hazards? What but disaster and hopelessness can easy virtue and a life of reckless abandon bring a society, a community, a family or an individual? How can a society be responsible when each time a girl/woman declares "I'm pregnant," the man who has showered her with inflated words of love and in whom she has invested her emotions, psychology and future can think of nothing better to say than scream: "I'm not convinced that I am responsible for it"? Is there a future for a society where it is normal for a girl like Njema to say: "Of course, men are all alike. They are so deceitful it may even tempt one to strangle them"? What does one make of a society where a girl would rather "simply commit simple abortion and put an end to everything" than tell the mother the truth of her pregnancy for fear that her mother would "make life unbearable" for her? What manner of society is this where a woman, to free one man of his sterility consciously deceives another man into believing that her pregnancy is not by him, however unfaithful, liar, cheat and opportunist the latter may be or however sincere the former is in his desire for a baby?

Seldom does Musinga, in his plays, leave his audience in doubt as to what the answers to the challenges of the moment or the way forward should be. In the case of *Njema*, his message to young girls is loud and clear: Since men are known to flee when trouble comes, leaving girls in misery and often in the hands of death, "If you have a lover, never mind the degree of the love, tell it all to your mother, tell it all to your father." The play ends with a voice urging all and sundry: "Abortion, stop it! It is infanticide. It is murder and in some unfortunate cases also suicide." Although this comes too late to save Njema, it is hoped that it comes in time to save others in similar predicament.

Kwo Victor Elame Musinga is a playwright preoccupied with social ills through themes articulating issues of morality, social justice, uprightness, corruption, callous indifference to public good, waywardness and the insensitivity of the haves towards the have-nots. In *An Invitation to God* and *Moka*, he addresses elitism and fair-weather friendship through the characters of Mandi and Ojoko respectively. To prove his majority as a Christian and earn recognition for years of service in honour of God, Mandi prays without relent for 79 days, inviting and pinning for God to come down and dine with him, but all in vain, as God, as usual gives his "sincere demand a deaf ear." This, Mandi cannot understand, as it is the very God that has promised all and sundry that whosoever asks, knocks and seeks fervently shall have their wishes granted. And granted God's omniscience and omnipotence, he has no reason to doubt. He blames God for being unconcerned and choosy, which he cannot understand as he is "rich in perfect love". Little wonder that he is "fearlessly and emphatically ... terribly disappointed" in God.

Just when he is about to give up in total frustration, God reassures him in a voice, accepting to dine with him, but on condition that "four different religious dignitaries [Cardinal, Moderator, Imam, Evangelism Secretary] as well as a lay personality" are invited as well. When Mandi assembles the guests as requested, a cripple appears, and in God's name, begs for food, much to the disappointment of Mandi who has "important personalities in here, expecting a Heavenly Guest at table." The cripple insists, "I go prayer God for you until you die," and "no God dey again pass me." "Massa give me food, and you dong give God food!" Mandi is impatient, and sends the cripple away in hunger.

After the cripple comes a blind beggar, followed by a little girl, both asking for food but in vain, because Mandi's food is reserved for God alone and the "very important personalities" he has asked to come along and join him at dinner with God. Mandi cannot see that God, his guest of honour, has taken the form of a cripple, a blind beggar, and a little girl, until a Voice tells him: "Mandi! Mandi! Mandi! Here I am again! You invited me to dine with you. I unconditionally accepted and both of us agreed on the day and time. (*Pause*) I called at your abode here three times within the agreed hour and most embarrasingly, you outrageously turned Me back three times. Despite My being the Guest of Honour and the fact that I told how hungry I was, my entire plea fell on deaf ears."

Most practicing Christians would be quite familiar with the theme of the play both from the Bible and the songs and sermons it has inspired over the years. The message is clear and compelling, one repeated by Jesus in many of his parables: whatsoever you do to the least of my brothers and sisters or creation, that you do onto me. When I was hungry, you gave me to eat; thirsty, you gave me to drink; homeless you gave me refuge; without clothes, you clothed me; lonely you kept me company; etc.; now come into the house of my father. And because Musinga's is a God of forgiveness not of punishment, a God of the masses not of the elite, a God for all and sundry, the Voice reiterates: "Earthly religious dignitaries, My ways are that of humility, gentleness and mystery for I am your God. I bless the food and as you eat, I am with you. Mandi, the Host of Hosts, Heaven is truly with you. Whatever you execute on earth is solidly ordained in Heaven."

In *Moka*, the theme of friendship is explored through the simple acts of dishonesty and greed, especially to those with whom one should be nothing but virtuous, open, generous and kind. Ojoko behaves in a similar manner to Mandi, by denying food to Esther her best friend, despite the discomfort and attempts at dissuasion of her house-boy. "I'm not here to be feeding others," she insists, and pleads with God in prayer to "command visitors, stop all visitors from coming to my house now, until I your servant Ojoko have finished my meal; then I can prepare to serve you once more, Amen." After the prayer she summons her food brought only to realize that it has been eaten by her own dog. This experience of disappointment by and in a friend, pushes Esther to reexamine her friendship with Ojoko, who has become "a pillar of ingratitude – Greed personified".Ojoko recognizes with regret that she has been pushed by her greed to "forfeit my best friend for good". Shamed by her behaviour, she tries to take it out on Moka, her long term houseboy, who would not take it lying down. In a song, he mocks at Ojoko, his Madam: "You lose your chop, Your lose your friend; You are full of shame, Cunny no good." As a veteran playwright and actor, Kwo Victor Elame

Musinga is more than just a pioneer in popular theatre. His simple but profound messages demonstrate a depth of understanding and insight into human nature and the nature of society. The texts he crafts are universal and timeless in their content and appeal, even as the themes and situations that inspire them are localized in specific places, experiences and histories. Kwo Victor Elame Musinga seeks to nurture, through his plays, the virtues of being human, while simultaneously crusading and inviting all and sundry to crusade against the dark side of humanity. In this regard he deserves to be celebrated as everyone's playwright, regardless of race, place, creed, culture, gender or generation.

Njema

Foreword

Everybody who is literate can read but not everybody who is literate can write, and attempt to write well too. More so, if it concerns one of these commonly talked about things - Love, Abortion. These often attract lots of criticisms as everyone who reads a piece of writing about them thinks they are competent to criticize and often think they know much more too. These criticisms are sometimes really constructive and are geared to achieving a positive result. Some are so bitter that they dampen the spirit of the writer and so scare those who would have been potential writers as well.

Mr. Musinga's courage to disregard such destructive criticisms has been shown not only in his determination to write, but also to choose to write on a difficult subject - Love, Abortion and AIDS. His effort must be commended and encouraged.

MBONG Nyansako-Ni-Ku (Mrs.)

Author's Introduction

Njema, the ill-fated adventure of a female student in love, condemns Abortion in its entirety.

Njema, the protagonist, is impregnated by her lover Aka, but he bluntly denies responsibility. She becomes worried and perplexed. Nevertheless, she confides in two girlfriends and asks for advice. Failing to trick an innocent admirer, Vicky, to accept responsibility, for the pregnancy, as advised by Eposi, and too scared to disclose her condition to her mother, she opts for abortion as advised by Liana. Njema however dies in the act. On her death bed, she advices her friends against abortion.

The mystery of her sudden death is revealed to her baffled parents by Liana following Njema's dying wish. "Abortion, Stop It! It is infanticide and in most cases also suicidal," a voice finally warns.

Many thanks to the Musinga Drama Group for popularizing this play on stage, to Mrs. Comfort Ashu and Mrs. Maria Bokossa for the pains they took to bring the play to this standard, as well as Mrs. Mbong Nyansako-Ni- Ku for writing out the foreword.

Attention

This play, presented to the public by the Musinga Drama Group, Buea, is now featured in the African Theatre programme of Radio Cameroon - Buea Station.

Victor Elame Musinga
September 1973

DRAMATIS PERSONAE

Njema, Female student and lover to Aka
Aka, Njema's unfaithful lover
Liana, Friend to Njema
Eposi, Friend to Njema
Vicky, Admirer of Njema
Tiki, Aka's secret lover
Kombe, Tiki's sweetheart
Teacher, Njema's class-teacher
Students, Njema's classmates
Father, Mother -Njema's parents
Mourners

Scenes

SCENE 1

AT NJEMA'S HOME -- 3.00PM

(*The curtain opens at the family home; the mother is clearly worried over her daughter's condition*)

Mother

All the same, my daughter Njema, I'm not happy at all; you are unusually dull and these days your breasts have suddenly shot up.

(*She moves into the room. Njema bolts the door, takes off her dress and examines her stomach and breasts in the mirror. She looks worried for a minute then recollecting something she smiles, dresses up hastily, looks for her books and remarks to herself*)

Njema

Aka is now waiting for me! I must be off!
(*She is about to go out when her mother calls from within*)

Mother

Njema? Fetch some drinking water from the public tap.

Njema
(*evidencing growing rebellion*)
Mama, this will make me late for evening classes.
(*Mother opens the door and holds a bucket to Njema*)

Mother

But there isn't a drop of drinking water in the house, and your father will soon return from work.

Njema
Mama, you mean that I must not attend classes because there is no water in the house?

Mother
Don't misunderstand me, my daughter. Go and you'll be back soon.

Njema
I'll be late and this will affect my lessons very badly.

Mother
If instead of arguing you had gone, you would now be on your way back.

Njema
Mama, you are only disturbing me. I'm going to school.

Mother

Njema, are you mad?

6

Njema

Mama, I'm in my full senses.

Mother

Look here Njema, I'll ask your father to stop paying for your education. It does not seem to be improving you in anyway.

Njema

(*Laughs out mockingly*)

That's nothing to me Mama. After all, I'm now a big girl.

Mother

(*Angrily*)

Njema, are your breasts deceiving you?

Njema

(*A little embarrassed*)

How and why? Mama, don't be jealous of me. I'm off.

Mother

(*Also embarrassed*)

Who is jealous of whom? Njema? Jealous of whom?

(*She calls out in vain, beats her breasts in disbelief, and calling on her ancestors to witness her shame begins to weep.*)

SCENE 2

A BUSHPATH

(*Njema can be seen in the embrace of a boy under a tree; they are so engrossed with each other her books drop and he tramples on them. They pull apart, she staggers in confusion, the young man supports her, helps her sit on the ground and he too sits by her; they converse intimately.*)

Aka

Njema, you're very warm, and you look sweet in this dress. Is this the latest style?
(*He offers her some sweets, biscuits and sweet drinks*)

Njema
(*A little excited*)

I hope you are not flattering me? (*Pause*) Aka, my mother always prevents me from coming out and...

Aka
(*Cutting in*)

Is she going to marry you?

Njema

Even now, she was putting all kinds of obstacles on my way; asking me to fetch some drinking water from the tap. I just put her in her right place and disappeared.

Aka
(*Clearly excited*)

Njems, I'll extract the poison of a live-snake. This will be the fuel that will keep the flame of our love burning.

Njema

Will our love then forever be as brilliant as the sun?

Aka

Surely sweetie! And even if the brilliance dwindles, the love will remain as constant as the stars. That is what our elders say.

(*They hug each other in exuberance, and return to their conversation, this time more intimately*)

Njema

Aka, I've always been praying that the hinges of our love should forever remain oiled.

Aka

This too, will be employed as the lubricant.

Njema

Aka, can you guess what has happened to me?

Aka

Now that we've hugged each other?

Njema

Not now!

8

Aka

What's it then? (*She gives him a bitter sweet smile, sighs and caresses him*) Please, tell me quickly. I cannot stand the suspense!

Njema

Aka, darling Aka …

Aka

I'm listening, Njems.

Njema

Aka, I'm pregnant with your baby.

Aka
(*in violent revulsion*)

What?

Njema

I'm two months pregnant.

Aka

You're not serious Njema.

Njema

Look how developed my breasts are. My mother has even remarked on them; she's quite observant.

Aka
(*A little confused*)

Is that the only symptom?

Njema

I've not experienced my menstrual flow for two months now.

Aka

For two months! Why didn't you inform me in the first month?

Njema

I thought it was as usual just late and expected the normal flow this month, unfortunately …

Aka
(*Cutting in vehemently*)

Say fortunately for you that it didn't flow!

Njema
(*Surprised*)

Why fortunate for me?

Aka
(*More angrily*)

Shut up! This cannot be true! You must be playing a game on me. Are you certain I am the father? (*Looking askance at her*) You must have been going around with another lover and that zygote is the result of your unfaithfulness.

(*He backs away from her.*)

9

Njema
(Frightfully embarrassed)

Aka, of all men, you call me an unfaithful girl?

Aka

Of course, through circumstances. And a zygote can be got! I through mere jokes.

Njema
(Sobs)

What are you saying Aka? Are you denying your responsibility for my present state? *(Pause)* O Aka, is this the brilliance or constancy that you promised even just a moment ago?

Aka

Have I yet extracted the poison from the live-snake with which to inflame our love?

Njema
(Pleadingly)

Please darling, go and extract it quickly and save me before it is too late.

Aka
(Sternly)

I will not dare it now! No! No! No!....

Njema
(Angrily surprised)

What! Aka.

Aka
(Unperturbed)

Njema, I'm not convinced that I am responsible for it.

Njema
(Dejectedly)

Aka, just visualize who you feel is responsible for this particular pregnancy.

Aka

It can be Aka, or some other person. All the same, Njema, let me go home before I misjudge, miscalculate and misfire.

(Aka goes off abruptly, leaving her in a desperate mood. In despair she falls to the ground and remains motionless under a tree.)

SCENE 3

AT SCHOOL

Njema's class in already in session, she is not in class and the lesson for the day is: Prevention of HIV/AIDS Virus and Pregnancy

Teacher
Precisely! Some of the signs to watch out for an HIV/AIDS patient are: Loss of weight; chronic diarrhea; chronic cough, itching and rashes all over the body. But these can be signs of other diseases. So, only an HIV lab test can confirm it.

Eposi
(Stands up)
Teacher, are there other ways besides sex through which the HIV/AIDS virus can be transmitted?

Teacher
For sure. I'll give you three most common ones; through blood transfusion with contaminated blood; by common use of syringes to administer injections on several patients; and the use of common toothbrush, especially among students.

Eposi
Can one be infected with this virus by a simple handshake with or hug from an AIDS patient?

Teacher
Eposi, that's a big NO. That is however a common misconception.

1st Student
By eating from the same plate or drinking from the same glass as an AIDS patient?

Teacher
Still NO.

2nd Student
By bathing together in a stream or from a bucket with an AIDS patient?

Teacher
Still not possible.

3rd Student
By sharing a seat in church, in a car or even here, in class, with an AIDS patient?

Teacher
(Emphatically)
No-way students!
(The students fears having been squashed they are perceptibly relived and give a high five to each response)

Liana
Please, why is sex so pronounced in the transmission of the AIDS virus?

11

Teacher

Because all across-the-board are actively involved in it; given that it is the only available source nature created by which the human race is increased. But some irresponsible people out only for fun indiscriminately move from one partner to the next and it becomes dangerous. They are aware of the risks but take no precautions and only realize when it is already too late that they are HIV/AIDS patients.

Eposi

Teacher, now that sex seems irresistible...

Class

(*In unison*)

Say it's really irresistible.

Eposi

Okay, now that sex is irresistible what can we, students, do to ensure that we do not contract the HIV/AIDS virus?

Teacher

This is the brightest question in this lesson. First, avoid friends who take you to places where conversations on and references to sex are frequent; especially the projection of sex-films. Second, stay away from all kinds of alcohol and drugs. As students, once you taste of any, irrespective of the quantity, you become dizzy, confused and unnecessarily bold; and will happily or unconsciously do anything demanded of you. In most cases, you give into sexual demands and only realize you're an HIV/AIDS patient when it is over.

Third, always occupy yourself by reading decent books, working, playing games and praying. Look, an idle mind is the devil's workshop and sex just for fun is the devil's action.

Last, and most important, practice abstinence and always offer a short prayer to God whenever the urge comes over you.

A Student

(*Explains*)

Abstinence, that is, we stay away from sex completely...

Class

(*in unison*)

Stay away from it completely! It is suicidal!

Teacher

Which do you prefer: to commit verbal suicide, like you've just done and still be alive; or engage in sex and commit real suicide?

Class

Teacher, how can we resist such temptation at our youthful age?

Teacher

In truth, sex is not something you students should concern yourselves with. The question of whether or not you're active should not even arise given that you are still

12

battling with your education and planning for your future. However, for your safety, if you have a strong urge, pray hard, then immediately discuss it with your parents in confidence. I mean your parents, repeat, your parents, and not with a close friend, a relative or someone in authority. Only your parents have your best interests at heart; whereas, others are liable to give you bad advice, lead you eventually to sex so that sooner or later you become either an HIV/AIDS victim or pregnant with a baby thereafter. Take note, they are all wolves in sheep's clothing when it comes to giving students honest advice on sex matters. Remember that AIDS has no cure yet. (*Pause*) Class, in all sincerity, any student serious about getting to the top of the education ladder and staying happily there to a ripe old age, should please stay away from sex until s/he gets married. But if the urge cannot be suppressed, stop your education and get married and enjoy safe sex. Look here, it'll be displeasing to God if you pretend to be studying when you've been infected with the virus through a clandestine sexual venture. You would have put your parents to an unbelievable financial burden only to die soon afterwards leaving them inconsolable. (*Pause*) The spike of a porcupine sharpens itself. With this breast-work of advice from me to you, let's now sing our AIDS song as we go home and remain committed to our promise to stay away from sex.

Class

No Madam. We are still confused about this abstinence.

(*Short silence. Clearly teacher is also confused and the class smiles. She comes to a decision. She brings out a photograph of a student who died some weeks back, then brandishes it before them and enquires*)

Teacher

You all know your former schoolmate Sophie who died some weeks ago. See how bulky and fresh she was when alive and well.

Class

What has that to do with our topic now?

(*They express sorrow and unhappiness about it.*)

Teacher

Did any of you see her when she was sick?

(*They shake their heads to signifying denial*)

Does anyone know what she was sick of? (*They still shake their heads*) Did any of you see her corpse?

Class

The corpse wasn't laid out in-state and no reason was given.

(*She now brings out another photograph of the same Sophie in full blown AIDS state and just prior to her death .*)

Teacher

Can you tell me who this is in this photograph?

(*They shudder with disgust, fright, unhappiness and complain.*)

Class

13

This is a horrible sight. Almost a skeleton from the grave. Is this a real human being created by God?

(Teacher places the two cards side by side before them and declares to their amazement)

Teacher

This is Sophie when she was well and alive, and this is the same Sophie when she was really sick and about to die. Class, Sophie died of AIDS. And so all AIDS patients die in agony, misery and with a disgraceful corpse.

(The declaration leaves the class in consternation. There is absolute quiet for one minute and then the students in turn declare)

Class

That was exactly why Sophie's corpse was not laid in state!

(They weep and damn the day AIDS came into existence; then curse anybody with the effrontery to approach and demand sex from them as long as they are students and unmarried. Spontaneously, they sing the AIDS song:

Abstinence or stay away from sex,
Never fails to prevent AIDS or unwanted pregnancy;
Abstinence or stay away from sex,
Ever prevents AIDS and unwanted pregnancy.

(They march out as they sing and disperse. Liana and Eposi walk along together singing.)

SCENE 4

A BUSH PATH

(Liana and Eposi are singing on their way home. When they get to a crossroad, Liana stops and demands)

Liana

Eposi, let's go this way and get Njema.
(They take the bush-path and converse as they go along.)

Eposi

You've just reminded me, Liana. Yes, I've not seen Njema in class for almost a week now and she has missed this lesson which was very educative for all of us.

Liana

Up to a week? What must she be doing? A few days ago I saw her somewhere having a good time with her darling Aka.

Eposi
(Surprised)

When she was supposed to be in class?

Eposi
(Diffidently)

I fear it's what the two of you are used to doing. It's nasty! *(Pause)* Let's hurry. It is getting dark.
(They approach the tree and as they perceive nobody at first sight, they look searchingly. Eposi points to something under the tree and enquires.)

Hey, what's that? Liana, is that not a human being under that tree?

Liana

Yes! Who can it be? No it cannot be! Not her! Not Njema!
(They scream, run to her aid and try to sit her up.)

Njema, Njema, where is Aka?
(Njema only sobs)
Have you been bitten by a snake?

Njema
(barely audible)

Yes, and by a very poisonous snake. Liana, I wonder if I'm going to survive it. I'm surely going to die.
(Eposi takes off her headscarf and folds it like a bandage)

Eposi

Where is the spot, so that we tie it up and stop the flow of poisonous blood into your heart?

15

Njema

Eposi, thank you. It's a poison, which cannot be carried by blood. It's the bite of a human snake. The poison was injected directly into my heart. It's too late.
(*They all sob*)

Eposi

But where's the darling you're supposed to be having a nice time here with?

Njema
(*Pathetically*)

He turned into a snake.

Liana
(*Frightfully embarrassed*)

Aka, changed into a snake?

Eposi

This is daylight wizardry! And to a sweetheart! Get up then. Let's hurry home before he returns to bite us as well.
(*They succeed to make her stand up, and then she explains*)

Njema

My friends, it is not the literal act of transformation and biting. (*Pause*) My sweetheart Aka has denied responsibility for my two months pregnancy. It's a nightmare.

Liana
(*More scared*)

Aka! Deny … Do not repeat it Njema! It sounds like a fairy tale!
(*Short silence*)

Eposi

It's no surprise to me. Men can do more horrible things than that.

Liana

I simply do not believe this. Do you mean to tell me that my own darling may one day treat me in such a manner?

Njema

Of course, men are all alike. They are so deceitful it may even tempt one to strangle them.

Eposi
(*Teasingly*)

Why don't you strangle Aka then?

Njema

He took me by surprise and…

Liana

… and completely paralyzed you!

Eposi

Certainly! That's the simple reason I don't have any tenant in my heart.

Liana

What are you Eposi? Do you yet understand a bit of what life is all about?

Eposi

Let me not understand it at all. You, who have a degree in life, solve this problem now for her. Come on, Miss Life!

(Short silence)

Liana

Don't mind her, Njema. *(Pause)* Now Njema, what can we do other than to employ the common means?

Eposi

Just a minute! Listen to my own suggestion. Now that it has happened, let her inform her mother of it and she will find a suitable solution to it. I fear, it's now a matter above our reach.

Njema

Eposi, my mother will murder me!

Liana

You are even going too far! Her mother will from thenceforth make life unbearable for Njema.

Eposi

If she makes life unbearable for you, she will be shamed at; if she murders you, which is impossible, she too will be hanged.

Liana

(Cutting in)

Let her simply commit simple abortion and put an end to everything.

Eposi

Which is simple abortion and which is not?

Njema

I don't fancy myself carrying that ingrate's child in my womb for nine months.

(Short silence)

Liana

Abortion is the best cure. I'll arrange for the most safe means. Let's sleep over the issue for some days.

(They are on their way home when Eposi brings them to an abrupt halt.)

Eposi

No! I don't agree that abortion is the final and best solution. There's yet another way out. Listen, look to one of your many admirers, as I am sure you have them in hundreds, and see which of them that you can foist this pregnancy on.

Liana

She should have them, since she engenders attraction that compels admiration even from the female sex.

Eposi

Yes, cling to one of them as the child's father and then cause him to take care of you till you put to birth; possibly after birth. *(Pause)* I want us to employ abortion as the very

17

last resort. After all, no one knows what this child may turn out to be in future.

Liana

(*Aggressively*)

It may turn out to be a murderer or a prostitute or...

Eposi

… or Njema's redeemer.

Liana

But who even asked you to come and offer such conflicting suggestions?

Eposi

The heavens asked me to come and save both of you from a serious crime.

(*Short silence*)

Njema

I now have two options before me. I'll try Eposi's, and if that fails, then I will carry out Liana's as the last resort.

Eposi

But I hope that by then I'll have another suggestion to make. However, good luck!

Liana

Whatever the situation and your decision let us hear from you in a week.

(*As they go out, Njema remarks*)

Njema

But as we depart, I'm thinking of Vicky who admires me.

(*They go out*)

SCENE 5

AT VICKY'S HOUSE - SIX DAYS AFTER

(It is evening. In a room with chairs and a well-dressed bed, magazines are thrown about the room. Silence. Soon, the door opens and a young man comes in with a girl by his side, She's Njema and he's Vicky)

Njema
(Made to sit on the bed she complains)
Vicky, I don't like our sitting on the bed every time I pay you a visit.
Vicky
(Joining her)
Being a fresh new darling, your generated current is speedily transmitted into me only when we sit on the bed,
Njema
But any of your visitors may be suspicious of us.
Vicky
(Offers her biscuits, sweets, Fanta)
This is my private apartment and your being here is my very private affair. *(Pause)* But after all, are we strangers to ourselves?
(Short silence)
Njema
Vicky, I just wonder why I consented to make love with you! I've always been aware of your advances to me, but doubted you sincerity.
Vicky
(Proudly)
I always rely on time. To me, every problem solves itself with time.
Njema
So the time is now come...?
Vicky
(A little excited)
...and along with you!

(A knock on the door)
Wait outside please.
(Vicky scarcely finishes answering when the door opens and Aka skips in. On seeing him, Njema frowns and Aka withdraws and disappears. Vicky is going to meet him outside when she warns.)
Njema
If you move an inch from here, I'll go away for good.
(He stays put and calls out)

Vicky

Aka, see you later. I'm too occupied now.

Aka

Thank you and bye.

(Short silence)

Vicky

Why did you react in such a manner?

Njema

Who is he to you?

Vicky

Only an acquaintance.

Njema

If he has any means of murdering me, he'll execute it hands down.

Vicky

(A little surprised.)

Why?

Njema

For almost nine months now, he has valiantly sought me for a girlfriend but I have repulsed him at every stage..

Vicky

I understand your stone-heartedness.

Njema

He is surprised at seeing me here.

Vicky

(Proudly)

And that places me above him in lovemaking.

Njema

(Cautiously)

Don't go making noise or he may grow jealous and cause my parents' to come to know of our affair.

Vicky

But who is he? A jobless fellow. A hanger-on.

(They hug and kiss. Short silence)

Njema

(Pretending intimacy)

Vicky, do you know that I have missed my menses?

Vicky

(Undisturbed)

Sorry!

Njema

Just that and nothing more?

20

Vicky

What else am I to do? Should I help you look for them?

(*He moves about the room as if searching for something when she drags him back to his seat and remarks*)

Njema

You men are funny.

Vicky

Funny? How? (*Pause*) We have barely made love for six days and all of a sudden you are complaining that you have missed your menses. You are instead funny.

Njema

(*Sobs*)

Vicky, are you denying responsibility for this pregnancy?

Vicky

Njema, it is too early to determine.

Njema

I understand. But you are also quick to deny it.

(*He gazes at her in wonder*)

Vicky

(Nodding in *Gradual in comprehension*)

Am I also denying it? (*Pause*) "Also" is now the word.

Njema

(*Struggles to divert it*)

My friend's lover has also denied responsibility for her present pregnancy, that's how the "also" came in.

Vicky

Both of you should then be a funny pair. One need not take any of you seriously. (*Pause*) Anyway, let me run after Aka and help trick him into your life...

Njema

(*Cutting in*)

So that?

Vicky

With the burning desire to have you, he'll accept any responsibility for your pregnancy no questions asked.

Njema

When you cannot accept, then you think he will?

Vicky

You never can tell where your luck lies.

Njema

Doesn't it lie with you?

Vicky

I fear it doesn't at all. Just a minute; let me hurry up and catch up with him before he

21

gets out of reach.

(Hurrying out)

Njema

No please, I don't admire him at all.

Vicky

It is now a matter of management.

Njema
(Desperately)

Vicky, let me manage it with you.

Vicky

Not me!

Njema

You won't find me here anymore on your return.

Vicky

That's all the same to me. Close the door on your way out. I'll inform you later of the results of my venture.

(He goes off; Njema bursts into tears)

Njema

Oh me! Have I any reason to live anymore? (Pause) I'm tossed from one devil to the other and then back to the same devil. A big girl like me! This is shameful, No! I cannot live to see all this. Let Eposi keep her fruitless advice. I will have to resort to abortion. And whether I live or die, it'll be all an experience. (Pause) Should I go and see Liana? (Pause) Yes, I think I will.

(She goes out determined.)

SCENE 6

AT TIKI'S HOME

(In the sitting room of Tiki's home, she can be seen plaiting her hair; Aka is on his knees before her pleading but she still tells him off)

Tiki

Aka, I'm not the Blessed Virgin Mary before whom you go on your knees to pray to.

Aka

Tiki, you are my Blessed Virgin Mary.

Tiki
(Embarrassed)

Aka, stop blaspheming. And now, I order you to get on your feet.
(He shamefully stands up)
I have told you that the baby I am carrying in my womb is not your baby.

Aka

I'll still be responsible for it, Tiki.

Tiki
(Astonished)

You mean you'll be totally responsible for someone else's baby?

Aka

That's exactly what I mean.

Tiki

You are kidding Aka.

Aka

I mean every word I say, Tiki.

Tiki

Aka, you aren't thinking of getting married to me, are you?

Aka

I'm marrying you today and forever.

Tiki

You have other girls whom you adore and care for; especially the young, fresh and juicy students.

Aka
(Laughs)

Yes, the other girls are tolerable but not pretty enough to tempt me into such a serious commitment. I go for the students just to enjoy their youthfulness. I will make no such commitment to a female student.

Tiki
(Laughs)

23

Now you're being emotional. Just leave me alone now.

Aka

Tiki, I want to leave here with a positive and encouraging statement from you. .

Tiki

What?

Aka

That I am responsible for this pregnancy.

Tiki

Aka, why this unusual concern about my pregnancy?

Aka

You have a well-to-do uncle who can assist when things go rough with us; and above all, Tiki, I think I profoundly and frightfully love you.

Tiki

(Taps off his hands)

Alright, I need some time to think this over.

Aka

(Anxiously)

How much time?

Tiki

(In a bit of a temper)

Aka, you'll hear from me. Please, you had better leave now as my uncle will soon be home.

Aka

That would indeed be an opportune meeting. *(Pause)* However, Tiki, my desires like my hopes are clear and high. Darling, help calm my troubled heart; let me hear from you soon.

(He has barely left when someone else slips in and hugs Tiki warmly.)

Tiki

Kombe, honey.

Kombe

(Joyfully)

Tiki, stories of my sterility have come to an end today.

Tiki

How?

Kombe

(Caresses her tummy)

You're now carrying my baby.

Tiki

(Surprised)

Kombe!

24

Kombe

Yes, I was at the door and overheard the entire conversation between you and Aka.
(*She places her hand on his lips to be quiet while he brings out a ring from his pocket and declares*)
Tiki, we are now engaged! (*Slips the ring on her finger; She admires it. They hug passionately, then she warns*)

Tiki

Kombe, let it remain our life secret that I consciously declared Aka's baby to be yours; simply because he is unfaithful, a liar, a cheat and an opportunist, whereas you are sincere in your desire for a baby.

(*They hug*)

SCENE 7

AT NJEMA'S HOME
MORNING

(The curtains are still down. From behind Njema can be heard chanting a sorrowful song)

Njema
I had a lover,
An illicit lover,
Out of my father's knowledge,
Out of my mother's knowledge.
He was that good,
Say as good as good;
'Twas out of my father's knowledge,
And out of my mother's knowledge.
He gave me gifts,
And also sweet kisses;
Which killed my moral knowledge
And sowed fast immoral knowledge.
(curtain opens and she is seen in bed twisting and turning in pain)

Now trouble is come,
He's gone and gone for good,
And leaves me in misery
And leaves me in the hands of death.
If you have a lover,
Never mind the degree of the love,
Tell it all to your mother,
Tell it all to your father.
(She screams out in pain. Almost immediately there is a knock on the door and Liana enters and expresses some fear on seeing her in bed)

Liana
Njema, how are you feeling? *(Pause)* Has it all come out?
(Njema only bends over in severe pains)
Are your parents gone to the farm?
(Njema only nods her head)
What's wrong, can't you speak?

Njema
(Gently)
Liana, I may not survive. I feel as if all the fires in hell are in my womb. I even find it

26

difficult to stand up.

Liana
(*Frightened*)

Don't exaggerate Njema. I hope I did not give you an overdose.

Njema

Maybe or maybe not. It would have been better I revealed it to my mother.

Liana

If you think it worthwhile, you can still tell her when it's over.

Njema
(*Diffidently*)

Liana, it may never be over and leave me alive. (*There is a knock on the door accompanied by a recognized voice. She turns to Liana*) That's surely Eposi. You go out by the back door and return later as if you are just entering lest she suspects me of having taken to your advice of committing...

Liana
(*Cutting in*)

... Abortion

(*She sneaks off to hide*)

Njema

Come in Eposi

(*Eposi enters and Njema pretends in vain to be cheerful. Eposi enquires*)

Eposi

You seem to be in severe pains, Njema. Has Liana been here?

Njema

No, she has not.

Eposi

Good luck! I feared she had already been here and administered *that* drug to you, since my first advice failed. Now that she hasn't yet come, listen to this other suggestion -- reveal it to your mother. She'll undoubtedly know what to do.

Njema

I've already done so.

Eposi

Just the right line of action. Has she thrown you out of the house, not to mention murdering you?

Njema

She has already administered it to me.

Eposi

What?

Njema

The abortion drug.

27

Eposi
(In confusion)

Your mother? But what then is the use of a mother to a daughter. *(Pause)* By the way, are you her real daughter or just a step-daughter? If you die, what would she say happened to you?

(Before she can finish, the door opens and Liana skips in, in high spirits.)

Liana

Njems, what's wrong?

Eposi
(In her engrossed ignorance)

Abortion! Her mother has already helped her to commit abortion.

Liana
(In pretentious ignorance)

There you are! Luckily, she did not take the advice from me.

Eposi

But she may not live.

(Short silence)

Njema

Eposi, please go and call my parents from the farm.

(Eposi hurries out and then returns)

Eposi

Have you heard the latest? *(Pause)* Aka is suffering from a slight mental disorder, and has tested positive to the HIV virus.

Njema
(Remarks)

That is as a result of his reckless sex life and the use of drugs.

(Eposi walks off sadly)

Liana, if Aka is an HIV victim, then I too have been infected. *(Pause)* Now, is there any longer any reason for me to live and then die later with a disgraceful corpse? No-way! Now is the best moment. *(Clearly in pain, she holds her stomach and weeps.)* Liana, this is my end. *(Liana starts weeping)* Do not weep. I don't blame you. You were only helping me as a friend. We've been friends right down to my grave. But you have to respect good breeding. I advise you to have only Eposi as your true friend. She is a good, conscientious girl in every way. *(Pause)* Do not reveal to anybody what has happened. Let them guess anything. And lastly, heed this advice:

> If you have a lover,
> Never mind the degree of love;
> Whisper in your parents' ears;
> Whisper to them frankly.

(She screams, stiffens up and dies. Liana is clearly petrified for some seconds, then she tries to wake her
28

up in vain. In fright and confusion, she screams and jumps about the room. The door crashes open as Eposi enters closely followed by Njema's father and mother. On seeing a motionless Njema, Eposi screams and the mother collapses. Njema's father is clearly devastated and confused. He quickly controls himself and warns.)

Father

Do not scream and alert neighbours. This is a death that can bring perpetual scandal to the family. Before any official post-mortem is conducted on the corpse, I'll like to know the real cause of her death. All of you should therefore be quiet while I go over to that village and get Mangamba the Powerful to unearth this mystery.

(He is about to rush out when Liana stands in his way and makes him sit down, then to the surprise of all present she speaks)

Liana

Departed spirit of my friend Njema, even though we both agreed under oath to have this as our everlasting secret, I have to reveal the cause of your death now and save your parents from premature death brought on by shock.

(Pause as the face of the corpse smiles, and then Liana begins the revelation.)

Njema's sweetheart impregnated her and bluntly denied responsibility for it. She was afraid to reveal it to you her parents.

Eposi
(Cutting in)

No! She just informed me she told Mama.

(The face of the corpse contracts severely at this remark)

Liana

No, she did not tell Mama at all. (*Once again, the smile is perceptible*) So her very close friend helped her to commit abortion, in the course of which Njema suddenly died. *(Pause)* Njems, please forgive me for revealing our secret. I hope you are not unhappy at the fact that everybody is now aware of the truth. (*The corpse remains smiling while the mother screams. Papa pulls Mama closer, makes the sign of the cross and remarks*)

Father

She has passed judgment on her dust.

Eposi
(Remarking)

Her hidden pleasures have become her parents' sorrows and open disgrace.

(Mourners come in)

Liana
(Advising)

> If you have a lover,
> Never mind the degree of love;
> Whisper in your parents' ears;
> Whisper to them frankly.

Voice

Abortion, stop it! It is infanticide. It is murder and in some unfortunate cases also suicide.

(Mourning song)

END

An Invitation to God

Introduction

Exhausted and disappointed on the 79th successive day at his failure to get the Almighty God to accept his invitation to dine with him here on earth Mandi castigates, lambastes and condemns God's unconcerned attitude towards his demand. He levies charges against God and finally declares there is no God. On this same 79th day, ironically, God talks to Mandi, fixes the day, place and time for the dinner, and requests the presence of some dignitaries of different religious denominations at the said dinner.

Does what happen to Mandi, from the moment God talks to him to the end of the episode, tie-in with the author's concept of God's form and being to be that of any human being; consequently, the good or evil, man metes on fellow man is meted on God?

A play for people of all walks of life, especially those in authority and for the spiritual and moral formation of the young.

The premier presentation of this play on November 7, 1999 in the Synod Hall Buea, by the Musinga Drama Group was in honour of the induction of the Moderator and Synod Clerk of the Presbyterian Church in Cameroon (PCC), the Rt. Rev. Nyansako-Ni-Nku and Rev. Dr. Festus A. Asana respectively.

Kwo Victor Elame Musinga

DRAMATIS PERSONAE

Mandi, Chief Host
Invitees:
Cardinal
Moderator
Evangelism Secretary
Imam
Lay Personality

God Incarnate:
Cripple,
Blind Beggar, God Incarnate
Little Girl

God's Voice
Place of Action: Mandi's House

SCENE 1

AT MANDI'S HOME

(*Someone can be seen on his knees muttering prayers. Soon a cock crows, then the wall clock strikes 6.00am. The man, Mandi, brings his prayers to a close and exclaims.*)

Mandi

My goodness! It's already dawn, and I have as usual been praying for three successive hours, with yet no answer! (*Pause, then disappointedly*) This cannot be true! I cannot understand why this should be so with the Good God. I just cannot understand. (*Pause*) Yes. Today is the seventy-ninth day since I've been praying you, Mighty God, very fervently, to accept my invitation to dine with me. The seventy-ninth day! I've been pining for you to leave your Up-high Abode for at least one hour and dine with me, your humble creature, down here. And yet, on this seventy-ninth day, you as usual give to my sincere demand a deaf ear. (*Pause*)

And Dear Lord, this demand, I make in keeping with your promise to mankind that whosoever fervently asks for whatsoever from you, will surely be granted their wish; and whoever knocks on your door, it will be opened unto him. (*Pause*)

My only God, haven't I knocked even harder than those unto whom you have opened with ease? Or haven't I demanded most sincerely and diligently? (*Pause*) Why then treat me with such a high degree of unconcern? Why, Good God? Or is it because I'm not rich in money or status; You're scared with the idea that I won't be able to give You and Your celestial entourage the lavish entertainment that those rich in money can? (*Pause, then diffidently*) God, you're a choosy God. But remember, if I'm not being egoistic, I'm rich in perfect love. Just the same stuff You're made of. (*Pause*) Or is my request clumsily worded? (*Pause, then damns it all*) But by the way, am I not stupid? Stupid to be addressing an invitation to the air with the firm belief that a Supreme Being can hear me! A Being I've never set eyes on or touched with my bare hands. And what is even more stupid, that I accept the Creature as my Creator! (*Pause*) Man, your hypnotic powers transcend the human race! (*Pauses, then in a loud desperate voice*) Omnipotence! Omnipresence! Omniscience! Are these not Your titles? (*Pause*) Whatever be it, I, yet with sincerity identify them with you. But note as I conclude this abortive demand, I fearlessly and emphatically declare that I'm terribly disappointed in Your Being. And finally God, if ever You see me on my knees calling on Your name again for whatsoever, christen me a bastard. Amen. (*A sudden wind is heard and felt in the room; then the rays of a strong light appear. Mandi calls out in fright*) O help! Where's this wind from? Help! Help! (*Pause*) And what's this ray of strong light? What's become of me, Mandi? O no, I can't stand it! Let me prostrate and protect my eyes, and wait for probably, my untimely death.

(*He prostrates in total surrender. A thunderous voice calls out*)

34

Voice

Mandi? Mandi? Mandi? Have no fear, but hear me. I am your rejected God. (*Pause*) Mandi, I have sorted out your thoughts and make this demand on you. (*Pause*) For seventy-nine days I have watched with undivided interest how this unique exercise and experience has frustrated you. (*Pause*) Mandi, your demand has found favour with me. So, I your God, will personally dine with you in this very earthly abode on the third day, from this day, and at the third hour precisely. (*Pause*) Invite four different religious dignitaries as well as a lay personality to dine with us. They are to bear witness to the fact that I came and will confidently propagate the message to the human race. Now get up and be confident. I'll soften the heart of every personality you'll invite to this dinner. Not one shall turn down your invitation. (*Dead silence*)

MANDI

(*In yet a frightened but hopeful voice*) Goodness gracious! What a frightening wind! What a thunderous Voice! What blinding brightness! And what magnanimity of the most High!
(*Fade out as he is chanting a glorious song*).

SCENE 2

STILL AT MANDI'S HOME
NEXT DAY

(A knock on the door; the door opens and some men enter in the following order)

MANDI

You're welcome. His Eminence the Cardinal, the Rt. Rev Moderator, the Evangelism Secretary, the Imam, as well as the Lay personality; Everybody invited is here and on time. God is mighty. Please be seated. *(Short silence)* Respectable men and women of God, let me express my profound appreciation to you for honoring this humble invitation of mine, the purpose of which is yet to be disclosed to you. All the same, I give praise to God Almighty for creating this situation. *(Pause)* Yes. The Omnipotence, Omnipresence and Omniscience who we all revere and adore, has accepted my invitation to dine with me here in my earthly abode tomorrow at this same hour.

(Pause as they look at one another in wonder)

At His request, I mean the Almighty God's, the invitation is extended to you to keep Him company at table and thereafter to testify to his attendance. *(Pause)* Respectable personalities, with this purpose revealed, I would also ask you to assist me to plan the menu and figure out my attire when I welcome Him to my humble abode. *(Pause)*. The ball is now in your court. *(Dead silence)*.

CARDINAL

Mandi, permit me address you: the host of hosts. ..

OTHERS

(In approval)

Sure! Sure! He is.

CARDINAL

Even though I'm a Cardinal and an earthly authority on Godly matters, the matter now on hand is that in which you are the final authority to instruct on what's to be done; since you're in full contact with the Man Up high.

MODERATOR

Earnestly speaking, this is a heavenly affair in which no other earthly religious authority is capable of giving even a nearly correct suggestion. I'm only here as a Rev. Pastor to listen and carry out instructions. Proverbially speaking, "The cobra cannot grow horns while the viper is alive." *(Silence)*

IMAM

Host of Hosts, whatever instructions you give out to us must be carried out to the letter, because, it's Allah command.

MANDI

Respectable personalities, I seem to have embarrassed you by my demand. I was trying

36

to abide by the saying that, "A roof carried by two will not be too heavy." However, I meant no harm. (*Pause*) May I then suggest that all traditional dishes one can think of on earth serve as menu for the occasion?

CARDINAL

I'll agree with you completely since tradition is closely related to God. I may add that the attire also be traditional. (*Short silence*)

EVANGELISM SECRETARY

The short silence indicates that the menu will consist of traditional dishes; and the Cardinal's idea of traditional attire for the host is also welcome.

MANDI

Will the Almighty not take me for a soothsayer if I'm clad in such attire?

MODERATOR

Host of Hosts be reminded that the Almighty is also All-knowing (*Short Silence*)

MANDI

Invitees, I don't intend to take up too much of your time. Understanding how busy you all are and since the essential points have been dealt with, I'll with your approval request that we bring this special meeting to a close.

CARDINAL

Gentlemen, I suggest that we move from here to the Archbishopric where we'll decide how to provide all the necessary traditional dishes and lay the table. Remember, we have barely twenty four hours to go.

MANDI
(*With confidence*)

God will provide all within the expected period. All the same, I wish you a successful deliberation.

LAY PERSONALITY

Please, can I come along with my camera to get the real image of the Supreme Being?

MANDI
(*Recollecting*)

You've just reminded me Lay Personality; the Most High is too bright to behold with the ordinary eyes that I advise each and everyone to put on a good pair of sunshades to help behold His face.

EVANGELISM SECRETARY

With this, I wonder how successful you'll make the snapshot.

IMAM

You never can tell where and when the Good Allah performs His miracles. After all, no venture no success.

MANDI

Until this same time here tomorrow, permit me, respectable personalities, to thank you immensely for honoring this invitation. Good bye!

(*They go away*)

SCENE 3

ON THE THIRD DAY - STILL AT MANDI'S HOME

(All the personalities are present, the table laid out with dishes and soft religious music plays in the background)

MANDI

Respectable invitees, all is now set for the great occasion of our dining with the Supreme Being. We need to exercise maximum patience for His arrival.

(Soon, they hear a knock on the door)

MANDI

Here comes the Mighty One!
*(Everybody adjusts themselves and stands up; **Mandi** opens the door and a **Cripple** is seen at the door.)*
MANDI
(In disappointment)

It's a cripple!

CRIPPLE

Massa, I beg you; for God name, help me, give me food. I de hungry plenty.

MANDI

Cripple, I've important personalities in here, expecting a Heavenly Guest at table.
CRIPPLE

Massa, I beg tie me the food for small paper make I go eat am for corner road; and I go prayer God for you until you die.
MANDI
(Laughing mockingly)

What God will you pray to for me, when the Supreme God will soon be here as my guest at table?
CRIPPLE

Lookam, no God dey again pass me. Massa give me food, and you dong give God food!

MANDI
(Angrily)

What ill-luck! A hopeless cripple impersonating God! *(Pause)* Invitees, this is just one of the temptations one is confronted with when one expects the Most Heavenly Guest.
(Closes the door with a bang)

38

CARDINAL

There is very high protocol even in heaven, as even the Almighty God Himself has observed in respect of this unheard of invitation. (*Pause*) That Cripple looks like the Good God's Harbinger.

ALL
(*In disapproval*)

God's harbinger? That's heresy, your Eminence! Downright ignominy to the Most High!

(Soon, another knock on the door)

MANDI

Ah here He is now. He has arrived!

(They all stand up, the door opens to disclose a beggar)

MANDI
(*In yet a disappointed tone*)

Now, it is a blind beggar! What is it? Let me warn you. Do not ask for food as you won't have it.

BLIND BEGGAR

Masa, I no di see place and I cam for beg you food weh na di only ting I want for dis ground. You get food plenty for your house but now you deny me.

MANDI

Yes, I've no food for you, bastard,

BLIND BEGGAR

Me, I di go, but member say, God no go give you anything weh you go ask from Him

(Goes away, Mandi bangs the door again)

MANDI

Hear that wretch! What other wish do I want to be fulfilled by God than to accept to dine with me. (*Pause*) Respected Invitees, if a third caller isn't our expected Guest, we'll call it quits and do justice to these dishes,

(Soon, there is another knock on the door)

ALL
(*In unison*)

And at last the Most High arrives!

(Mandi opens the door)

MANDI
(*Loud and angry*)

It's a little girl

GIRL

Sir, do you have a party here?

MANDI

Yes, and so what?

GIRL

I'm terribly hungry and have been waiting for this party all this while. Can you please put some crumbs of food on a plate for me to fill my stomach with?

MANDI
(*Surprised*)

The party has not started yet. But who are you lass?

GIRL

Simply dish me a bit of everything at the table; thereafter, I'll disclose my identity to you.

MANDI
(*A little angry*)

Are you ordering me! Lass, I don't care whoever you may be, but I deeply sympathize with your poor upbringing.

GIRL

Sir, to ask for food is no mark of poor upbringing. (*Pause*) Look here sir, I'm hungry, you've invited persons to dine with you, and now you talk rubbish!

LAY PERSONALITY
(*Angrily*)

Mandi, what a blockhead you are to argue with a little rat, and keep important personalities waiting for a heavenly visitor. (*Pause*) Just get a whip and chase it away.

MANDI
(*In approval*)

I think you're right. Let me look for a whip,

GIRL
(*Going off*)

Let the God you are waiting for come and dine with you. I'm off.
(*Goes off*)

LAY PERSONALITY
(*Aside*)

As a layman, I think this situation a pure hoax. How did this fellow, Mandi, successfully convince us to believe that God Himself would come to earth and dine with us! This is witchery.

MANDI
(*Calmly*)

Respectable Invitees, with all solemnity, I declare that we do justice to these dishes while hoping for the arrival of our Guest. May His Eminence lead us in prayer?
(*The Cardinal barely comes to the end of grace before meals when a sudden wind is heard and felt in the room. Pause, then the ray of strong light appears.*)

ALL
(*In confusion*)

Oh help! We are all dead men! Where's this wind from? Mandi help us! (*Pause*). And what bright blinding light is this? This is pure witchcraft. We are all dead men.

MANDI
(*Commanding*)
Everybody should fall prostrate and be silent. Here at last comes the Almighty God!

(*They fall down on their knees, silence, then a thunderous unearthly voice calls out*)

VOICE
Mandi! Mandi! Mandi! Here I am again! You invited me to dine with you. I unconditionally accepted and both of us agreed on the day and time. (*Pause*) I called at your abode here three times within the agreed hour and most embarrassingly, you outrageously turned Me back three times. Despite My being the Guest of Honour and the fact that I told how hungry I was, my entire plea fell on deaf ears.

(*Pause*) Mandi, I take criticism cheerfully and forgive cheerfully. Also be reminded that any incessant, fervent and worthy demand of Me is always fulfilled. But watch out for the time and manner of fulfillment. (*Pause*) Mandi, I was the Cripple. (*Pause*) The Blind Beggar was still Me; (*Pause*) and the Little Girl was yet Myself. (*Pause*) Mandi, I feel your profound remorse and for that I forgive your misbehaviour. (*Pause*) Earthly religious dignitaries, My ways are that of humility, gentleness and mystery for I am your God. I bless the food and as you eat, I am with you.

(*Dead silence then they get on their feet*)
ALL
(*In unison*)
Mandi, the Host of Hosts, Heaven is truly with you. Whatever you execute on earth is solidly ordained in Heaven.

(*They go into a song of praise to God*)
MANDI
Respectable invitees, let's fill our sacks with this blessed food.

(*They eat and chat*)
MODERATOR
Mandi has proven one earthly and perhaps also heavenly principle; that "a hunting dog's rattle can't be silent until the animal is killed."

IMAM
As long as you breathe this free air, never cease to pray to Allah.

CARDINAL
Yes! Any fervent prayer is surely answered; but the time and manner of answering are unexpected.

EVANGELISM SECRETARY
Any spectacular happening in man's life is God's plan. (*As they rise Mandi remarks*)
MANDI
Respected and God-fearing personalities: "The human being with whom man interacts

41

in life is incontestably God Himself."

ALL

Host of Hosts!

LAY PERSONALITY

O my camera! I forgot to take that snapshot!

(They all laugh out)

(Fade out as they chant a lively song)

END

Moka

Introduction

Lady Ojoko, simultaneously and dramatically forfeits the love of her best friend, Esther; her delicious meal to a dog, and respect from her long-time houseboy, Moka.

Now, read or watch this piece on stage and learn why this rare fate befalls Lady Ojoko and what lessons lie therein for the young and old alike.

DRAMATIS PERSONAE

LADY OJOKO, *Full of greed and unfaithful friend to Esther*
ESTHER, *Sincere friend to Lady Ojoko*
Moka, Houseboy of Lady Ojoko

DOG.
Place of action: Lady Ojoko's Residence.

AT LADY OJOKO'S RESIDENCE
(NIGHT)

The curtain opens in the sitting-room of Lady Ojoko; she is about to have a light supper. She is interrupted by a knock on the door and she hastily covers the dish; in a low voice she calls for the houseboy

OJOKO
(Calls)

Moka? Moka?

(A shabbily dressed fellow enters and she signals him to clear the table quickly and then open the door for the visitor. He does so deftly; as he opens the door she pretends to be doing her hair. Door opens and her best friend, Esther, enters, rubbing her stomach with her hand as if in pain and subsides onto the sofa. Ojoko enquires as Moka looks on)

OJOKO

Bo Esther, what's wrong with you?

ESTHER

Ojoko, I've not eaten since this morning and there's no food in my house.

(Ojoko shakes her head in sympathy)

And as you're aware, my darling Okosko no longer provides me with food money since I scolded him for humiliating you in public. But what's his food money to me where you're concerned! Please, get me any pot-luck to fill my empty sack.

OJOKO

Weh Esther, what hard luck. I've just finished eating and there's just nothing in the house left to offer you. Again, this stupid Moka didn't inform me this morning that there was no food in the house

(Moka who stands facing Ojoko, signals her to the food he just cleared from the table and she signals him back to be quiet. Then standing, Ojoko sends him away as she whispers to him)

Do not say there's some food in the house.

(He goes out and she resumes her seat)

ESTHER

Ojoko, let me have some fresh water to drink.

OJOKO
(Calls out)

Moka? Moka? *(he comes in)* Bring some water for Esther.

(Moka does not understand what has been demanded of him)

MOKA

Engine wata?

(Ojoko mimes the act of drinking and only then does he understand. He hurries out and returns with a large bowl of water which he holds over Esther's mouth. To his amazement she gulps down all of it. He goes out)

ESTHER

Ojoko, this water has actually refreshed me. Let me go home now.

OJOKO

Let Moka see you off since it is dark and I'm getting ready to go out with my darling.

ESTHER

No, that is not necessary. I'll go alone.

OJOKO
(Insists)

You can't go out alone in that darkness. *(Calls out)*. Moka? Moka? *(He enters)* See off Esther. *(Moka clearly does not understand what is demanded of him. Ojoko has to mime the act of seeing off someone. Only then does he understand; he goes in and returns having changed into a funny getup and goes off with Esther. Short silence, then Ojoko breaks it)* Am I safe to have asked Moka to see off Esther? He's such a talkative fellow he may unwittingly disclose to her that there's some food at home. *(pauses)* What miscalculation! No, I'll call them back *(she calls out)* ESTHER? ESTHER?

(Esther responds from a distance)

ESTHER

Ye-e-e-s.

OJOKO

Esther, I've just recollected that this area is habitually visited by thieves, and to leave the house with nobody after I have also gone out would be very risky. So, let Moka come back.

ESTHER

All right. He's coming back and good night.
*(Soon Moka returns to **Ojoko's** great relief and she immediately orders him)*

OJOKO

Serve my food. I'm not here to be feeding others.
(He understands "food" for foot and sets to take off her shoes when she mimes the act of eating, then he goes for the food, serves it and looks on as she makes a short prayer)

O God command visitors, stop all visitors from coming to my house now, until I your servant Ojoko have finished my meal; then I can prepare to serve you once more, Amen.

(Moka joins in the "Amen" and goes out in wonder as she begins to eat. However she has hardly started to eat when there is a knock on the door. She hastily covers the dish rebuking God awhile) O thoughtless God, why a contrary answer to my most fervent prayer. The more I pray, the less fulfilled are my wishes.

(She then calls out and Moka enters and she signals him to clear the table and open the door. He is going to open the door with the dish in his hand when she quickly intervenes. He takes the dish in and returns to open the door. As Esther again enters, Moka in total disgust goes off without welcoming her)

OJOKO

Esther! What is it again! Anything the matter?

ESTHER

Nothing. Just that it's terribly dark out there...

OJOKO
(Cutting in)

And you need the flashlight?

ESTHER

That's it.

OJOKO
(calling out)

Moka? Moka?

(He comes in)

Bring the flashlight on the small table for Esther.

(Not until she mimes the working of a flashlight does Moka hurry out for it. Soon, there comes from within, the harsh scream of a dog in great pains. Shortly thereafter, Moka enters with the flashlight and Ojoko enquires)

OJOKO

Moka what happened to the dog?

MOKA
(Unconsciously revealing all)

Madam, the dog chop all the chop you tell me to hide as Madam Easter enter. So I vex plenty and give the dog one big kick like this:

*(He demonstrates the kicking action on the wall, then on the table, soon on the chairs as Ojoko, in vain, signals to him to keep quiet and go out. Disgusted, Ojoko forces him out while he is still trying to explain what happened. Meanwhile Esther is dumbfounded by this revelation. In shame, **Ojoko now** turns around and belatedly asks to Esther)*

OJOKO

Bo Esther, Let's have a bite,.

(After a short silence, Esther exhales deeply in wonder, then castigates her)

ESTHER

O Ojoko, is it mere food that must separate us! Is it just food Ojoko! I opened my heart to you, but this is what I receive: abject ungratefulness. *(Pause)* Where's my Ojoko? Where's my heart? Where's my heart of gold? *(Pause)* I see instead, before me, a pillar of ingratitude. Greed, personified! (*Pause*) Let me go home before I collapse here; there'll be nobody here to give a true account of my situation. However, I no longer need your flashlight for the night is now bright. Good-bye my one-time acclaimed heart of gold.

(*Ojoko is tongue-tied as Esther sorrowfully walks out; Moka runs after her and calls out in vain*)

MOKA
(*Calls*)

Madam? Madam Easter? Good friend for my Madam? Take flashlight. I no deny you flashlight.

(*Esther goes off and he turns to Ojoko*)

Madam, what is matter with you friend Easter, and dog, and chop, and me and flashlight?

OJOKO
(*Castigates*)

Shut up! You damned, stupid, thoughtless blockhead, and talkative impostor in the Republic of Ignoramus. Madam, I kicked the dog like this: (*Here she gives him a hard kick which sends him crashing onto the floor*) And that should've been all of your response. But that you went on to duplicate your response, and further multiplied the duplication with further explication. (*Pause*) And this duplication and multiplication have not only exposed my greed but also caused me to forfeit my best friend for good. (*Pause*) No, this is too bitter a pill for me to swallow. I must pay you back in a similar coin. (*Pause*) Now Moka, you are dismissed from my service; that's, you are no longer the houseboy of Lady Ojoko. Get out of my house!

(*Moka weeps and does all to touch her heart in vain. Then he summons up courage and rebukes her in this song*)

Moka
(*sings*)

You lose your chop,
Your lose your friend;
You are full of shame,
Cunny no good.

Refrain:
O Madam,
Cunny no good (twice)
From now you must
Know well,
That cunny no good.

(*Angered, she chases him about the room with a stick as he sings and he finally rushes out*)

END